FRANK COLQUHOUN is a former Canon Residentiary and Vice-Dean of Norwich Cathedral. Previously, most of his life was spent in South London, where he was for seven years Vicar of Wallington an . subsequently Canon and Chancellor of Southwark Cathedral and Principal of the Southwark Ordination Course. Now retired, he lives at Bexhill in Sussex.

His many books include *Parish Prayers, Contemporary Parish Prayers* and *New Parish Prayers.* He is also editor of the revised edition of the BBC service book, *New Every Morning.* His previous publication for Triangle was *Prayers that Live.*

Family
Prayers

Compiled and edited by
Frank Colquhoun

TRI△NGLE

First published 1984
Triangle
SPCK
Holy Trinity Church
Marylebone Road
London NW1 4DU

British Library Cataloguing in Publication Data

Colquhoun, Frank
  Family prayers.
  1. Prayer-books
  I. Title
  242′.8   BV245

  ISBN 0-281-04103-2

Typeset by Pioneer, East Sussex
Printed in Great Britain by the
Anchor Press, Tiptree, Essex

Contents

Preface

The prayers that make up this short collection are designed
in the main for use in the family circle or house groups
rather than in public worship. They are of mixed character
and style and cover a wide range of subjects; and these
factors will, I hope, increase their usefulness and broaden
their appeal.

The book consists of old and new material. I am
particularly grateful to the following who have contributed
new prayers: the Rev. Richard Bewes, the Rev. Llewellyn
Cumings, Bishop Timothy Dudley-Smith, Mrs Helen Lee,
Canon John Poulton, and Sister Phyllis and Sister Susan of
the Community of St Francis. I also wish to thank the Rev.
Richard Harries for allowing me to include several prayers
from his *Praying Round the Clock* (Mowbrays, 1983). The
majority of my own prayers have been written specially for
this book.

Grateful acknowledgement is made to the Episcopal
Church of the United States of America (ECUSA) for
prayers from its revised *Book of Common Prayer* (1977); to
the Mothers' Union for prayers reproduced or adapted from
The Mothers' Union Prayer Book and *The Mothers' Union
Service Book*; to Mrs Joy Whyte for two prayers adapted
from her *Prayers for a City* (London City Mission, 1978);
and to Canon D. W. Grundy and Canon F. W. Street for
their prayers.

In the Index of Sources an asterisk (*) has been added to
the ascription of prayers which have been altered or
shortened. I hope that in no case I have ascribed prayers to
wrong sources or infringed any copyrights.

FRANK COLQUHOUN

*Family
Prayers*

1 Let us Pray

What is prayer?

1

Before we pray, let us remind ourselves of what true prayer
is: the lifting up of our hearts and minds to God.
>   We adore him and glorify his name;
>   we confess our sins and ask to be forgiven;
>   we thank him for all his mercies;
>   we pray for others and for ourselves;
>   we listen to him and seek to know his will;
in the name of Jesus Christ our Lord.

Teach us to pray

2

> Lord, teach us how to pray aright,
>   With reverence and with fear;
> Though dust and ashes in thy sight,
>   We may, we must, draw near.
>
> God of all grace, we come to thee
>   With broken contrite hearts;
> Give, what thine eye delights to see,
>   Truth in the inward parts;
>
> Faith in the only sacrifice
>   That can for sin atone;
> To cast our hopes, to fix our eyes,
>   On Christ, on Christ alone.
>
> Give these, and then thy will be done;
>   Thus, strengthened with all might,
> We, through thy Spirit and thy Son,
>   Shall pray, and pray aright.

The open way

3

Heavenly Father, we come to you in the greatness of your love and lift up our hearts in prayer and praise.

We thank you that the way to your presence is always open through Jesus Christ and that you invite us to draw near in full assurance of faith.

Help us to pray simply and sincerely, unselfishly and gratefully, remembering the needs of others as well as our own, and giving thanks always for all things in the name of Christ our Lord.

In touch with the Infinite

4

Lord, grant that prayer may be to us no routine exercise or burdensome duty but an amazing privilege: our entering into communion with you, the living God, our Creator, our Father, our Redeemer.

When we pray, we, mere creatures of time and space, are actually in touch with the Infinite.

Help us to grasp the wonder of it, and so to experience its reality that our whole life may be spent in unbroken fellowship with you in the Spirit; through Jesus Christ our Lord.

The spirit of prayer

5

Give us grace, Almighty Father, to address you with all our hearts as well as with our lips.

You are everywhere present: from you no secrets can be hidden.

Teach us to fix our thoughts on you, reverently and with love, so that our prayers are not in vain, but are acceptable to you, now and always; through Jesus Christ our Lord.

Listening

Lord God, when we pray we believe that in your love and mercy you are listening to us, for you delight to hear the prayers of your children.

Help us also when we pray to listen to you: to quieten our hearts, that we may hear the still small voice of your Spirit speaking to us as we reflect and meditate in your presence.

Open our inner ears to hear what you are saying to us; and then give us grace to receive your word and to respond in ready obedience, in Jesus' name.

Where two or three ...

We thank you, Lord Christ, for the promise of your presence to the two or three who gather in your name.

Help us to remember that you are with us now as we meet together to pray.

Make us of one heart and mind, that we may agree in what we ask; and as we ask in your name, so may we pray in accordance with your will, and glorify our Father in heaven.

The Lord's Prayer: a simple paraphrase

Loving Father of us all,
    transcendent in glory,
may all people honour your holy name
    and acknowledge your kingly rule,
that your purposes may be fulfilled on earth
    as truly as they are in heaven.
Give us today all things that we need
    for our material and bodily wants.
Forgive us the wrong we have done,
    and make us as ready to forgive others.

Save us from yielding to temptation
    and falling into sin;
and rescue us from the forces of evil
    at work around us and within us.
For you, O Lord, are sovereign over all things;
your power is sufficient for all our need;
to you be the glory now and for ever.

Prayer as a five finger exercise

9

I start with the *thumb* — it's nearest to me; so I pray for
those who are closest in my affections and thoughts. I lift
them before you, Lord, watch over them today.

Next, the *forefinger*, which points and gives direction.
And so I pray for those who have authority over my life: my
teachers and instructors; my parents; my pastor . . .

Then the *big finger*. Let me pray for those in important
positions: the Queen; the Prime Minister; the leaders of the
nations; the heads of industry; local government.

And the *fourth finger?* Pianists call this the weak finger;
so I remember in my prayers the weak and the vulnerable;
the sick in body or mind; my elderly neighbours; the
homeless and the unemployed.

Last of all comes the *little finger*. That stands for me.
Thank you, O Lord, for including me in the circle of your
great love. You know my needs and I am content to leave
them in your care.

2 *Giving Thanks*

For the love of God

10

God our Father, we can never thank you enough for your
great love for us made known in your Son Jesus Christ:
  the love that redeemed us and all mankind at so great a
    price;
  the love that freely forgives us and welcomes us into the
    family of your Church;
  the love that watches over us day by day and will never let
    us go;
  the love that is stronger than death and from which
    nothing can separate us now or ever.
God of love, accept our thanksgiving and give us grace to
love you more, for Jesus' sake.

For the redemption of the world

11

We praise you, O God, that in the greatness of your love
you sent your only Son to redeem mankind:
  to break the tyranny of sin,
  to overcome the power of death,
  to open the kingdom of heaven to all believers.
We thank you for your Church throughout the world
proclaiming this great redemption, and for the vast company
of the redeemed who join with us in singing the Redeemer's
praise.
Accept their praise and ours, O God,
and may all glory be yours
this day and every day
and to all eternity.

For God's Providence

12

Heavenly Father, as we look back over the years we thank you for your wise and loving providence in the ordering of our lives.

There were times, we confess, when things seemed to go wrong and we suffered disappointment; but we are grateful now that plans we made were frustrated, that hopes we cherished were unfulfilled, that prayers we offered were not answered as we wished.

We have learned that your ways are better than ours, and that in all things you work for the good of those who love you.

So we give you thanks; and in simple trust we commit all our future days to your sovereign will, in the name of Christ our Lord.

For God's many gifts

13

Father of all mercies, we offer you our thanks for all the gifts you have so freely showered upon us.
> We thank you especially for health of mind and body,
> for home and family and friends,
> for books and art and music,
> and for the bountiful world in which we live.

Help us to use your gifts wisely, faithfully and generously, that we may show our gratitude in our deeds and not in words only, and glorify you in our lives as well as with our lips; through Jesus Christ our Lord.

14

Almighty God, we lift up our hearts in thanksgiving for your rich and varied gifts:
> for the life you have given us;
> for health of mind and body;

for the beauty of the world around us;
for the order and constancy of nature;
for the loveliness of the changing seasons;
for the fruits of the earth and for our daily bread.
God of all grace, for these many blessings may your name be
praised; and with all your gifts grant us also thankful
hearts, for Jesus Christ's sake.

For all that is good

15

Thank you, Lord, for all that is good:
satisfying work and innocent pleasure,
contentment and affection.
For all that is fulfilling,
for all that warms us through,
for all that is strong and healthy,
we bless your holy name, O Lord.

For the gift of life

16

We bless you, O Lord, our Creator,
for the life you have given us,
the life you have sustained and preserved,
the life that is ours now.
We thank you for the bodily powers which enable us to
enjoy life,
for all the gifts of mind and spirit which make life
worth living,
for the glorious life to come in your eternal kingdom.
Lord of our life, accept our thanksgiving,
and let our days always be spent in your service
and used for your glory;
through Christ our Lord.

For the gift of health

Make us always thankful, our heavenly Father,
    for the precious gift of health;
for our sight, our speech, our hearing;
    for all the powers of body and mind
        through which we can enjoy life to the full.
Teach us to look after the health we have;
    deepen our compassion for the sick;
and help us with thankful hearts
    to use our health and strength
    in your service and to your glory;
through Jesus Christ our Lord.

For the beauty of the earth

We give you thanks, most gracious God, for the beauty of
earth and sky and sea; for the richness of mountains, plains
and rivers; for the songs of the birds and the loveliness of
flowers.

    We praise you for these good gifts, and pray that we may
safeguard them for posterity.

    Grant that we may continue to grow in our grateful
enjoyment of your abundant creation, to the honour and
glory of your name, now and for ever.

Lord, I have seen the sky today
painted on rain-swept streets,
watched through the roof-tops the slow march of clouds,
silent and splendid.
I have seen rainbow colours on a starling's wing;
and on the wasteland of a demolition site
a spire of willow herb making the grey day bright.
And as night falls, the dark polluted river
in its black-walled bed will be alight with stars.

Lord, for your deep-reflected loveliness
which all our crowded artifacts cannot conceal,
for your majesty and power and infinite artistry,
I bow in spirit and give praise to you.
Always, everywhere, your gracious touch is evident.
Your own resurgent life is never crushed
or hidden far from sight.
O Lord my God, for all the glory of your universe
my heart sings praise to you
each day I live.

20

O God, the maker and giver of all good things, we praise
you for your creation and for our capacity to enjoy it.

Enable us to see your hand in all the beautiful things
around us, and from them to learn something more of your
greatness and glory, your wisdom and love. For Jesus' sake.

For our homes

21

God our Father, in these days when so many people are
homeless refugees, we should be grateful for our homes.
Make us truly thankful for them and for all that they mean
to us;

> for the peace and security they give us, and
> for the family life they enable us to enjoy.

May they be places where others find a blessing as well as
ourselves; for Jesus Christ's sake.

For friendship

22

Lord Jesus, thank you for being our friend and for enriching
our lives with so many gifts of your love.

Thank you too for human friends and for all they mean to
us.

We thank you especially for those who have helped us and stood by us in difficult times.

Help us, who have received so much, to give true friendship to others, in your name and for your sake.

For the arts

23

Praise God for his precious gifts of music and art, drama and poetry, and all creative skills.

Praise God for books and literature.

Praise God for every means by which our lives are enriched and inspired.

Praise God who alone is worthy of all praise; for from him, and through him and for him, are all things; and to him be glory for evermore.

For books

24

Father, we thank you for the gift of language and for the printed page.

We thank you for the books that have helped to shape our lives and to mould our tastes and values; that have furnished our minds, spoken to our hearts, enriched or entertained us, both in health and sickness.

Teach us to value the written word and to use it rightly; through him whose words are words of life, our Saviour Jesus Christ.

For our talents

25

We thank you, our Father, for the varied talents you have given to your children: to some the gift of music or painting, to others of writing or athletic skills.

Above all we thank you for the gifts of friendship, sympathy and understanding which can bring help and happiness to others.

Show each of us what are your special gifts to us, and enable us to use them for your glory; through Christ our Lord.

Remembering the departed

26

Heavenly Father, we thank you for those we love who are now at rest in your presence.

Today we remember especially — and thank you for the life *he* lived, the work *he* accomplished, and for the example *he* left behind.

We praise you that death can never finally separate those who love Jesus, and that at last we shall be reunited in the Father's house and be for ever with the Lord.

General thanksgivings

27

Accept, O Lord, our praise and thanksgiving for all that you have done for us.

We thank you for the splendour of the whole creation, for the beauty of this world, for the wonder of life, and for the mystery of love.

We thank you for the blessing of family and friends, and for the loving care which surrounds us on every side.

We thank you for setting us tasks which demand our best efforts, and for leading us to accomplishments which satisfy and delight us.

We thank you also for those disappointments and failures which lead us to acknowledge our dependence on you alone.

Above all, we thank you for your Son Jesus Christ; for

the truth of his word and the example of his life;
    for his steadfast obedience, by which he overcame
        temptation;
    for his dying, through which he overcame death;
    and for his rising to life again, in which we are raised to
        the life of your kingdom.
  Grant us the gift of your Spirit, that we may know him
and make him known; and through him, at all times, and in
all places, may give thanks to you in all things.

28

O God of love, make us more thankful
    for all the boundless mercies of our daily life.
Forgive us that we are so often ungrateful,
    complaining and discontented,
taking for granted your greatest gifts:
    the blessings of health,
    the comforts of home and family life,
    the joys of friendship,
    the wonders of your creation.
Teach us day by day to number our blessings
    and to receive each one as from our Father's hand;
and fill our lives with gratitude,
    our lips with praise;
for the sake of Jesus Christ our Lord.

3 Marriage, Home and Family

Christian marriage

29

God our Father, who made men and women to live together
in families: we pray that marriage may be held in honour;
that husbands and wives may live faithfully together,
according to their vows; and that the members of every
family may grow in mutual love and understanding, in
courtesy and kindness, so that they may bear one another's
burdens and so fulfil the law of Christ; for his name's sake.

30

Almighty God and Father, we thank you that you created us
male and female in your own image, to share in your divine
life and to fulfil our high destiny in marriage.

Help us to recognize the sanctity of the marriage bond,
and to see in the love of man and woman a mirror of your
everlasting love; through Jesus Christ our Lord.

For a married couple

31

Almighty God, giver of life and love, bless — and —. Grant
them wisdom and devotion in the ordering of their common
life, that each may be to the other a strength in need, a
counsellor in perplexity, a comfort in sorrow, and a
companion in joy.

And so knit their wills together in your will, and their
spirits in your Spirit, that they may live together in love and
peace all the days of their life; through Jesus Christ our
Lord.

A wife's prayer for understanding

32

O God, our heavenly Father, in marriage you entrust us to each other: give me an understanding heart, so that I may not fail your loving purpose for my husband.

Help me to heal, not hurt; to encourage, not destroy. In you and through you may we become what you would have us be, grown whole together. And this I ask in thanks to you, Father of tender wisdom, Father of perfect love.

The birth of a child

33

Heavenly Father, how good you are!
How wonderful are your works!
We praise you for all your gifts
and especially for your gift to us
    of this dear child.
We take *him* to our hearts
and welcome *him* to our home
    as a token of your love;
and gratefully we give *him* back to you,
to love and serve you all *his* days,
    in the name of Jesus our Lord.

34

Heavenly Father, creator and giver of life, there is such joy in our hearts at the news of a baby's birth,

    a most special and complete gift of your love,
    a new being and a wonder of creation.

Be with the mother and father of this little baby in their happiness, and accept their praise and ours as we give thanks to you, through Jesus Christ our Lord.

The adoption of a child

Loving Father, you understand our longing for children and as we approach the adoption of this child — we seek your guidance and help.

We know that all children are only gifts on loan from you, and no more the possession of natural parents than of those who adopt them.

Help us to accept this child as one who is infinitely precious to you; save us from regarding *him* as less than a natural child; and grant that both *he* and we may grow to full maturity in your kingdom, where all are equally yours and members one of another.

We ask this in the name of Christ our Lord.

Our children

36

God of love, we pray for our children as they grow up in our family circle.

Give us understanding of their needs, and show us how best we can help them as they face their problems and prepare for the life of the world.

Help us to establish a relationship of trust between them and ourselves, and to make our home a place where at all times they may find love and security; in Christ's name.

37

God our Father, we ask your blessing
on the children of our family,
and on those for whom we have responsibility.
Grant that they may grow up
healthy and strong, wise and good,
in the knowledge of your love
and in the service of your Son,
Jesus Christ our Lord.

Heavenly Father, you have blessed us with the gift of children and trusted them to our care.

Give us the understanding and patience we need as we bring them up, that we may lead them in the way of Christ and teach them to love whatever is just and true and good, for the glory of your name.

39

Merciful Father, we pray for our children
in their life at home and at school.
Watch over them and protect them from evil;
guide them into the ways of your will;
and prepare them for their work
in the life of the world;
for the sake of Jesus Christ our Lord.

Teenagers

40

God our Father, we pray for our young people growing up in an unstable and confusing world.

Show them that your ways give more meaning to life than the ways of the world, and that following you is better than chasing after selfish goals.

Help them to take failure not as a measure of their worth but as a chance for a new start.

Give them strength to hold their faith in you, and to keep alive their joy in your creation; through Jesus Christ our Lord.

41

Father, we commit to you the young members of our family as they go out into the world and are exposed to the snares and temptations of a materialistic society.

Help them to distinguish between life's true values and the false, between that which builds up and that which degrades, that they may choose to follow not what is popular or easy, but only what is right and good.

Lord, have them in your keeping. We have done what we can for them; now we leave the rest to you. One thing we know: they cannot pass beyond the reach of your love and care.

42

Lord, give us patience!

We know that our children will have different tastes from us in their friends and pastimes, in music, clothes and many other things; and yet it is so hard to accept that our own ways are not always better than theirs.

Help us to recognize and affirm all that is good and positive in them; and give us the wisdom to know when to speak and when to be silent.

And while we know that they must learn from their own mistakes, save them from mistakes that will hurt them or others spiritually; for your great love's sake.

The Christian family

43

Father of all, accept our thanks for the joys of family life.

Help us to live so that we may strengthen and enrich the life of the family.

Help us to build with you the kind of family which welcomes the stranger, the lonely and the needy.

Teach us through this small family to love the family of all mankind and to realize our part in it.

In the name of Christ we ask this.

44

Heavenly Father, we bring to you in our prayers
    all whom we love in our family circle,
knowing that your love for them
    is so much greater than ours,

and that your will for them
  is all that is for their good.
So have them in your keeping, O Lord,
  and give them now and always
  the fullness of your blessing;
  for Jesus Christ's sake.

45

We thank you, our Father, for all the blessings you have given us as a family. Continue to watch over us all day by day and keep us in safety of body and soul.

We pray for the children, that they may grow in grace as they grow in years; and for the older ones that they may know your will and purpose for their lives.

We remember loved ones now absent from us; and those who are ill or anxious or sorrowful, or in any kind of need, especially —.

God of love, hear our prayer and answer it as you see best, for the sake of our Saviour Jesus Christ.

One-parent families

46

Loving Father, we ask you to bless fathers and mothers who are alone in bringing up their families.
  Guide and strengthen them when they are beset by doubts
    and difficulties;
  help them to lead their children to know and love you;
  and assure them of your presence at all times; for Jesus
    Christ's sake.

The home

47

God our Father, whose love for us is eternal and unchanging: help us to make our homes patterns of your love:
  places of mutual trust and forgiveness;

18

places of true sharing and caring;
places of deep joy and peace;
and unite us all one to another in the circle of your love, in
Jesus Christ our Lord.

48

O God, whose Son prepared to save the world by sharing
the life of an earthly home: help us as a family to love and
serve you as we care for one another's needs; and give us
those blessings which will enable us to make our home
more worthy of your presence; through Jesus Christ our
Lord.

49

Heavenly Father, whose Son Jesus Christ,
    born of a woman,
sanctified the life of an earthly home:
bless the homes and families of our nation.
Give to parents a true sense of responsibility
in the care and training of their children;
that our boys and girls may grow up
    in the fear of your name
    and the fellowship of your Church,
for the glory of Christ our Lord.

Those we love

50

Heavenly Father,
whose eternal, perfect love can shine
even in our fragmented, fleeting relationships:
bless all those to whom we are bound
by ties of kinship and affection.
Bind us to one another and to you,
through him in whom dwells the fullness of your love,
even Jesus Christ our Lord.

Young and old

O God, you have granted to youth to see visions, and age to dream dreams: help both young and old to understand each other.

May those who are young be courteous to the aged; may those who are older look with sympathy upon new ideas; so that both young and old may work together for the coming of your kingdom, to the glory of your name.

Absent members of the family

Heavenly Father, you are present everywhere
and care for all your children:
we commend to you the members of our family
who are now parted from us.
Watch over them and protect them from all harm;
surround them and us with your love;
and bring us all at last to that home
where partings are no more;
through Jesus Christ our Lord.

God of all grace, we commit to your care those we love who are absent from us. May your presence surround them and your peace be in their hearts; and while we are parted from one another join us closer together in your love; for the sake of Jesus Christ our Lord.

In a time of temporary separation

Heavenly Father, beyond whose love and care we cannot pass, bless — as *he* leaves home, and keep *him* in safety and peace.

While we are parted may we never forget that, though separated by distance, we are still united in your presence; and may we be bound to one another in love and prayer until we meet again; for our Lord Jesus Christ's sake.

A marriage in the family

55

God our Father, whose greatest gift is love, we ask your blessing on — and — as they prepare for their wedding.

May the love and trust they cherish for each other be constantly deepened;

may nothing ever come between them to break the harmony of their marriage or the peace of their home;

and through all the changes and chances of life may they be drawn closer together and closer to you.

We ask it in the name of Christ our Lord.

56

Lord, help us to begin our life together as we hope to go on and to cherish the love that we have for each other, knowing that it comes from you.

Guide us into that oneness of life that is your promise to every husband and wife.

Bless our marriage, dear Lord, that in it we may find true joy and fulfilment; for Jesus' sake.

Grace at meals

57

Thank you, Father, for food, family, friends, and for all your blessings, in Jesus' name.

For these gifts of food, and for your loving care for us day by day, we thank you, our Father, in Jesus' name.

Give us grateful hearts, our Father, for all your mercies, and make us mindful of the needs of others; through Jesus Christ our Lord.

4 Life's Changing Scenes

Moving house

58

O God, you lead your people as a shepherd leads his flock: we thank you for your mercies to us while we have lived in this area, for friendships made, for joys and sorrows shared.

Be with us as we move to our new home, and direct us into fresh avenues of service.

Teach us to venture trustfully into the future, while we retain our gratitude for the past.

Above all, make us to live each moment in ways pleasing to you and in obedience to your will; for the sake of Jesus Christ our Lord.

The blessing of a new home

59

Lord, bless this house and all who live in it.
Hallow it with your presence and your peace.
Let it be a place where prayer is made,
    where love abounds,
    where your name is honoured;
and may your fatherly hand be over us day by day,
    in our going out and coming in,
    now and for evermore.

Leaving home for the first time

60

Heavenly Father, we ask you to bless — as for the first time *he* leaves home and family and friends.

Help *him* to know your love and constant presence wherever *he* is, and protect *him* in mind and body.

Fill *him* with the power and joy of your Holy Spirit and keep *him* faithful to your Son, Jesus Christ our Lord.

Starting work

61

God our Father, whose Son began his adult life in the carpenter's shop at Nazareth: we remember before you — and all who are setting out upon their working life.

Enable them to see their work as part of your creative purposes, even when it is dull; and save them from assuming that work is an evil to be finished as soon as possible, or something to be done simply for the sake of money.

Uphold them when their faith is tested; keep them true to their Christian convictions; and direct all their way ahead in life; for Jesus Christ's sake.

Daily work

62

Lord Jesus Christ, we thank you that you have taught us, by word and example, the dignity and sanctity of all honest work.
Help us in our daily duties to follow in your steps:
to be faithful in whatever we undertake,
to give always of our best,
and in all things to act as your servants;
to the glory of God the Father.

The unemployed

63

Heavenly Father, we remember before you those who are out of work, especially your servant —. Support *him* and *his* family in this time of anxiety; and guide us as a nation so to use our public and private wealth that all may find suitable and fulfilling employment; through Jesus Christ our Lord.

Retirement

Father, help me to use this added gift of time
wisely and well, unselfishly.
Help me to turn to profit the experience
of all my toiling life. Not for myself
but for some other's good. The health I have,
help me to treat it with respect. And over all,
give me a cheerful heart to live each day
with laughter and with thankfulness.
Yes, praise the Lord, my soul!

Lord, as my working days come to an end, I thank you for
the years of work you have given me, and for bringing me
now to this time of retirement.

Help me to accept it graciously and to adjust to the new
pattern of my days.

Keep me still interested in life; still of service to others;
still finding something to do; still learning; and still happy
to the end; through Jesus Christ our Lord.

Old age

Lord Jesus Christ, you are the same yesterday, today and for
ever and you have promised to be with us all our days: we
pray for all elderly people, especially those who are ill or
house-bound, and particularly —.

In their weakness may they find your strength, and in
their loneliness know the joy of your presence; and be to
them a sure and certain hope of the life that you have
prepared for them in the heavenly home; for your love's
sake.

Lord, we do not know how much of life
   is left to us in this world,
for you have veiled the future
   from our eyes.
But we know that all our days are in your hand
   and that no one can snatch us from your keeping.
Your mercy has never failed us throughout our life,
   nor will it fail us at the end.
So as we praise you for all that is past,
   we trust you for all that's to come,
in the name of our Saviour Jesus Christ.

Sunshine and shadow

68

God our Father, we live in a world of sunshine and shadow.
Help us to accept that fact and not to expect life to be all
sunshine.

May we remember that the sun is still shining even when
we cannot see its light, and that it is the sunlight that
creates the shadows.

So may we know that your love, like the sunshine, is
unceasing and unchanging, and learn to trust you in life's
darker hours as well as in the light; for Jesus' sake.

In anxiety and uncertainty

69

O God, you know how worried and anxious we are at this
time about . . .

Help us to be calm and unflustered, and keep us trustful.

When we have done all that is in our power, enable us to
be patient and to leave the rest to you.

Above all, give us the certainty that you are with us in
our trouble, that we may know your peace which the world
cannot give and can never take away; for your love's sake.

70

Heavenly Father, you know us better than we know ourselves,
so we need not tell you how perplexed we are.
Human advice often seems so shallow,
and we don't know what to do.
Help us to see our present situation through your eyes
and to relate it to your wider purposes.
Keep us from worrying over trivialities;
show us step by step what to do next;
and strengthen our faith in your ability
ultimately to bring good out of all that happens.
In Christ's name we ask it.

Waiting

71

God our Father, it is hard to wait. I realize that much of life
is taken up with those 'in-between' periods, waiting for
something to happen, waiting for news, waiting for the letter
that never seems to come. And now here I am, waiting again.

May this waiting period strengthen me as a person.

May your friendship and love transform this from being an
empty experience without meaning into one of purpose and
growth.

May I look back one day, grateful that I found in you the
motivation and the power — to wait.

72

Heavenly Father, we lift up our hearts to you in this time of
anxiety.

We thank you that we can bring all our troubles and
problems and lay them at your feet.

Deepen our faith, and draw us nearer to yourself, that we
may find your grace, your guidance, and your peace. For
Jesus' sake.

Difficulties in marriage

73

Loving Saviour, you taught us that all things are possible to our heavenly Father.

Strengthen our belief in your words, especially in the difficult days of our marriage when fears, mistrust and doubts arise.

Renew our spirits with fresh awakenings of love, joy, trust and forgiveness; that by your grace our marriage may be restored to its former harmony, and together we may give you thanks and praise.

Disharmony in the family

74

Forgive us, Lord, when jealousy, greed, temper or pride disturb the peace of our family. Help us to find the right words and actions to soothe and heal the hurt.

Forgive us when we quarrel, and make us ready to forgive one another; and may harmony be restored to our married life, and peace rule in our home; for the sake of Jesus Christ our Lord.

Marriage breakdown

75

We remember before you, Lord, those whose marriages are at risk or have broken down.

You alone know the story behind each unhappy and broken marriage.

We remember especially just now — and —.

Make them willing to recognize where they may be at fault; give them a sincere desire to put things right; and teach them in their desperate need to turn to you, whose love is unfailing and whose power can make all things new, in Jesus our Lord.

The divorced

76

O Lord, we pray for those who, full of confidence and love, once chose a partner for life, and are now alone after final separation. May they receive the gift of time, so that hurt and bitterness may be redeemed by healing and love, personal weakness by your strength, inner despair by the joy of knowing you and serving others; through Jesus Christ our Lord.

Loved ones in need

77

Heavenly Father, we bring to you in prayer: — and — and . . .

In simple trust we commit them into your hands.

We thank you that you love them more than we do and understand their every need.

Do for them, O Lord, what we cannot do, and what you see is most for their good; for Jesus' sake.

78

God of love, graciously hear our prayer for those in need: the sick and suffering, the lonely and the bereaved, especially — and — . . .

Help them each one to look to you in their trouble, that they may receive the strength and peace which you alone can give, through Jesus, our Saviour and Lord.

79

Father, remember in your mercy those we know who are in particular need of your help.

Grant healing to the sick in body or mind.

Comfort the sorrowing and anxious.

Give patience and courage to the elderly and lonely.

And may your peace be with them all, this day and every day, for Jesus Christ's sake.

Illness in the family

God our Father, with faith and love we remember before you our dear — in this time of *his* illness.

We bring *him* to you in the confidence that you love *him* and know *his* every need, and that your healing power is still the same today.

Bless all that is being done for *his* recovery, and answer this our prayer as you see best, for the sake of Jesus our Lord.

81

Dear Lord, we feel the ache of anxiety when one of the family is seriously ill. We confess that we find it difficult to settle, or to concentrate on anything else, until we know the outcome.

Teach us that you are just as active and involved as we are; and help us to see that in your fatherly care and watchfulness you are far ahead of us already.

Deal with the ache in our hearts and give us grace sufficient for each day. For your name's sake.

For one in hospital

82

Our loving Father, from whose mighty hands
all life and healing come,
have now within your own intensive care
this suffering one dear to us.
Give sleep tonight, give peace of heart,
and freedom from anxious fear,
that healing may be quietly at work.
And since there is oneness in the face of sickness,
let this your servant have an open heart
to lift the hope of others who are there:
to show that love of yours
which never lets us go, nor ever fails,
wherever we may be, whatever pain we suffer.

The dying

83

We pray, O Lord, for your servant — whose life is drawing near its end.

Give *him* your peace in *his* heart.

May *he* know the Saviour's presence with *him* and rest *his* faith wholly in Him; that through your redeeming love *he* may enter into your eternal joy and join the heavenly host who live and praise you for evermore.

The mentally ill

84

Heavenly Father, we remember to our comfort that you have in your special care all broken, outworn and imperfect minds.

Give to those who live with them and minister to them the understanding and loving Spirit of Christ.

Enlighten those who are tempted to laugh at such illness or regard it with shame; and to all who are thus separated in this life by barriers of mind, grant the peace and consolation of your Holy Spirit; through Jesus Christ our Lord.

85

God of love, we bring to you in the name of our Lord Jesus Christ those who are suffering from mental illness, and especially . . .

In your mercy heal their sickness, dispel their darkness, and make them to know that you are ever near them, their loving Father and unfailing friend; and give them peace.

In time of bereavement

86

God our Father, in our sorrow today we look to you for the comfort and peace that you alone can give.

Grant us the assurance that you are with us now, and that

in perfect wisdom, perfect love, you are working for the best.

Help us to think not of the darkness of death but of the splendour of the life everlasting in your presence; and in your mercy strengthen and uphold us until we meet again those we have loved and lost awhile; through Christ our Lord.

87

Dearest Lord, you wept for Lazarus your friend, and your heart was filled with sympathy for the widow of Nain.

Hold in your loving arms those who now mourn, and surround them with your quiet comfort.

Show them yourself as the Resurrection and the Life.

Soften the pain of their loneliness by the assurance of your nearness; and let your love which conquered death flow into their hearts and fill them completely, now and for ever.

88

We hold in your presence, O God, those who mourn.
Unlock their hearts that they may grieve truly;
Open their minds that they may find
a new direction in their lives;
and grant them the comfort of your presence.

89

Almighty Father, you understand the secrets of every heart: strengthen and sustain those who know the sorrow of bereavement.

May they experience the comfort of the Holy Spirit within them and the love and fellowship of the church family around them; and may they see before them the hope of glory, beckoning and leading them to their true home and the moment of reunion in your heavenly kingdom; through Jesus Christ, our living Saviour and Lord.

Lord, this dreadful thing has happened, and our minds are baffled, our spirits weighed down with grief.

It is beyond our understanding why this little life should be taken, or why we should be called upon to suffer so terrible a loss.

Yet we know that life is full of mystery and that many others at this time are facing the same problem and enduring the same anguish as ourselves.

Help us to bear our sorrow without bitterness, and not to question your love; for to whom can we look for comfort but to you, O Lord?

Speak your word of peace to our hearts; ease our pain and lift our darkness; and be to us a very present help in trouble; for Jesus Christ's sake.

5   The Local Community

Our neighbours ✓

91

Heavenly Father, we thank you for our neighbours and for
the people around us with whom we share our daily lives.
   We pray for those who are old and lonely;
    those isolated because of ill-health;
     and those who find it difficult to make friends.
Show us what we can do to help, and teach us to be good
neighbours; for Jesus' sake.

92

Jesus, you said we should love our neighbours as ourselves.
Help us therefore
       to love ourselves,
       to accept ourselves,
       to cherish ourselves,
       and to be gentle with ourselves,
in order that we may
       love others,
       accept others,
       cherish others,
       and be gentle with others,
for love of you.

93

Help me, Lord, to be more like you:
to draw a circle that includes rather than excludes.
Give me a genuine love for others,
both those I like and those I don't like.
Help me to overcome my fears and prejudices
and to see your image in all men.

Our friends

94

Most gracious Lord, we thank you for the gift of friendship and for all those with whom our lives are joined in true affection.

Teach us to value our friends and to regard each one as a gift and token of your love.

Make us ready to extend friendship to others and to remember the housebound, the lonely, and those who need a friend's helping hand; for Jesus Christ's sake.

Community life

95

O God, you have set us in a society where we are free to select our own values; no one can force us to believe.

So give us grace to choose wisely.

Help us to reject the shallow, the artificial, and the trivial.

May we rediscover those deep things on which our life together depends.

96

Thank you, good Lord,
for the rich variety of human society;
for diversity of race and colour and background.
Help us to recognize our differences
and to accept them with love and laughter.
Unite us and all things in yourself that
the fullness of your glory may be set forth.

Caring for others

97

Thank you, O God, that you have made us in your own image and given us the potential to become more and more like you.

Help us to fulfil the law of our being by coming to care for others as deeply as you care for us; through Jesus Christ our Lord.

98

Father, you have given me
   an abundance of energy.
Please help me to use it
   for the benefit of others,
especially the deprived
   and the underprivileged;
for the sake of your Son,
   Jesus Christ my Saviour.

Ministry to the sick

99

God of all grace, we ask your blessing on the work of doctors and nurses, and all who tend the sick, in the hospitals and nursing homes of this neighbourhood.

Strengthen them for their tasks, and give them the joy of knowing that they are furthering your own purposes of love and healing, in Jesus Christ our Lord.

Our schools

100

Loving Father, we ask your blessing on the schools of this area.

We thank you for those who give their lives to teaching the young. May they do their work as a service rendered to children and young people in your name, and constantly endeavour not only to impart knowledge but to build character, and to equip those they teach with a firm faith, a courageous spirit, and a true sense of values; for Jesus Christ's sake.

Those who serve the community

101

God our Father, we remember with gratitude those who in their different ways serve our community.

We pray for those who guard the public health and minister to the elderly, the sick and the infirm;

those who care for the young and those who teach in our schools;

those who serve in local government, administer the law, and preserve the peace.

Assist them in their varied duties, and deepen within us all the spirit of loving service; through Jesus Christ our Lord.

The urban community

102

Heavenly Father, strengthen our resolve to make Christ known in this town [city].

Help us to recognize the struggles of those who feel oppressed by their urban environment.

Help us to fight against the pressures that threaten to dwarf and dehumanize the individual.

Help us to protect and strengthen the quality of family life.

And help us to create, where we are, a community that anticipates the life and harmony of the heavenly city, whose architect and builder is God; in the name of Jesus Christ our Lord.

A prayer for peace

103

Give peace in our time, O Lord:

peace and reconciliation among the nations;

peace and unity within the churches;

peace and harmony in our communities and our homes;

peace and love in all our hearts;

for the sake of Jesus Christ, our Saviour.

6 The Church Fellowship

The local church

104

Thank you, Lord, for our local church:
for those who have worshipped in it over the years
and for those who serve it today.
Grant that all who enter its doors
may be enabled to renew their relationship with you
and may find your peace, your strength, your grace,
and above all your presence.
Help us as a congregation to be outward looking,
so that what we find within our fellowship
we may share with those outside,
for the benefit of all and for your greater glory,
in Jesus Christ our Lord.

105

Lord God, we thank you that the church here is part of your
whole Church throughout the world, and that in our faith
and worship we are united to all in every place who confess
the name of Christ.

Keep us always mindful of the greatness and richness of
the fellowship to which we belong; and make us more
worthy to follow in the steps of the saintly and heroic
company who have gone before us in the way of faith, to the
glory of your name.

Before worship in church

106

Heavenly Father, draw near to us as we draw near to you
now in this hour of worship.

Open our hearts to receive all that you have to give to us,
and graciously accept all that we have to offer you, in the
name of Jesus Christ our Lord.

O God of peace, you have taught us
that in quietness and confidence
    shall be our strength:
in our worship lift us to your presence,
where we may be still and know
    that you are God;
through Jesus Christ our Lord.

Holy Communion

Father, we pray that our communions may never be mere
routine but always precious times of fellowship with Jesus
Christ as we thankfully remember his redeeming love and
meet with him as our living Lord.

   May we come to your table with joyful and expectant
hearts, and go out afterwards nourished and strengthened
in spirit to serve you in the world, to the glory of your name.

Come to us, Lord Jesus, in your risen power
when we receive the bread of life
and the cup of salvation.
Cleanse our hearts from sin,
    that they may be worthy of so great a guest;
and keep us abiding in your love,
for your great name's sake.

Lord Christ, who said 'Do this in remembrance of me': help
us at every Communion service
        to look back, and remember your death for us on the
        cross;
        to look up, and know that you are the risen Saviour in
        our midst;

to look around, and rejoice in our fellowship with one
   another;
and to look forward in hope to the coming of your
   kingdom and the heavenly banquet.

The baptism of a child

111

Lord Jesus Christ, we thank you for your love for little
children.

When you were here on earth, you welcomed those who
were brought to you, took them into your arms and blessed
them.

May your blessing be upon our dear child — whom we
bring to you in baptism, to be received into the family of
your Church.

Grant that *he* may grow up to be a faithful member of
that family, and may learn to love and serve you all *his* days;
for your name's sake.

Confirmation and church membership

112

O God, you prepared your disciples for the coming of the
Spirit through the teaching of your Son Jesus Christ: make
the hearts and minds of your servants ready to receive the
blessing of the Holy Spirit, that they may be filled with the
strength of his presence; through Jesus Christ our Lord.

113

We thank you, our God and Father, for those who have
made confession of their faith and have been welcomed into
the communicant life of the Christian family in this place.

Help us by our prayers, our friendship and our example to
encourage them in the way of Christ, that they may grow up
into him and go on to serve you in the worship and
fellowship of the Church, to the glory of your name.

114

Give us, dear Lord, the modesty to know that the work in which we are engaged is but a part of the obedience of your whole Church.

Give us faithfulness to fulfil that part by being all that we are meant to be and doing what we are meant to do.

And give us the enthusiasm to share the task with those whom you have called to serve in other ways, that together we may proclaim your great salvation; through Jesus Christ our Lord.

Sharing the gospel

115

Heavenly Father, you have called your Church
    to proclaim the gospel in all lands:
help us in obedience to your call
to participate actively in the Christian mission
    in our own country and overseas,
and to commend the gospel of Christ
    by what we are,
    by what we say,
    and by what we do for others,
to the glory of your name.

116

O God, we pray for the sharing of the good news of Jesus Christ in this neighbourhood, throughout our country and across the world, and for our part in this; that Jesus Christ may be so presented in the power of the Holy Spirit that many may come to put their trust in him, to accept him as their Saviour and serve him as their King in the fellowship of the Church; for the honour of your holy name.

A Bible study group

117

Dear Father, as we gather round your Word
we pray you to bless us with your company.
Give us a hunger for the bread of life;
open our minds to all the searching truth
and healing comfort that are here for us.
Open our hearts to you, our present Lord;
open our ears to one another,
that we may be enriched by others' insights.
And make us obedient, Lord,
that we may hear, and understand, and go from here
to do your perfect will with confidence.

118

Risen Lord Jesus, who opened the minds of your disciples to
understand the scriptures: we ask you to open our minds
now and to give us the same understanding as we study the
Bible together.

May your Spirit direct our thoughts and make the Bible a
living book to us, so that in the printed word we may find
you, the living Word, our Saviour and our Lord.

Stewardship

119

Jesus, Lord and Master,
teach us to follow the pattern of your manhood,
that we may learn to interpret life
in terms of giving, not of getting;
to be faithful stewards of our time and talents
and all that you have entrusted to us;
and to take every opportunity
of serving the needs of others
and advancing your kingdom in the world,
for the glory of your name.

Lord Jesus Christ, you have taught us that much will be required of those to whom much is given, and that all our possessions are a trust from you.

May we be faithful in the exercise of our stewardship and generous in the use of money, and learn that it is more blessed to give than to receive, according to your word; for your name's sake.

Possessions

Lord Jesus Christ, you have taught us that true life is not made up of the amount of things we own.

Write this word on all our hearts today.

Save us from the sin of covetousness, from the love of money, from the materialistic spirit of the age.

Help us to keep our minds fixed on the things of eternal value, the things that money cannot buy; that we may store up riches in heaven, and may know that even now, in possessing you, we possess the true wealth of eternal life.

7 Our Leisure Hours

Use of leisure

122

O God, in the course of this busy life give us times of refreshment and peace; and grant that we may so use our leisure to rebuild our bodies and renew our minds, that our spirits may be opened to the goodness of your creation; through Jesus Christ our Lord.

123

Thank you, my Father,
  for quiet moments in the rush of life:
    time for my inner self,
    time to look back with thankfulness,
  time to notice the gifts of yesterday —
    a leaf, a cloud, a lighted window,
    bread on the table, fire and water.
For this short space, Lord,
    take from me the bustle and the stress;
and fill me with joy and peace
    in believing;
  through Jesus Christ our Lord.

124

We thank you, O God,
    for times and seasons;
    a time to work
    and a time to rest.
Thank you for leisure,
    for space to savour life
    and recreate ourselves
    in change and freedom;
and for the fun of holidays.
Let nothing spoil your gifts
    to us this day;
  for Jesus Christ's sake.

Use of time

Eternal Lord God, may we never forget that we are accountable to you for what we do with our time.

Save us from misusing it or idling it away.

Teach us to make the most of it, while it is ours; that we may know how best to use it for your glory, the benefit of others, and our own eternal welfare; through Jesus Christ our Lord.

Taking rest

Lord Jesus, you invited your disciples to come apart and rest awhile, and you yourself were glad to relax by the well of Sychar in the heat of the day.

You understand our human nature and how tiredness affects many people:

mothers with small children and many chores,

fathers with heavy responsibilities,

young people with lots of homework.

Help us all to make time in our lives for adequate rest, that we may be relieved of strain and renewed in strength; for your name's sake.

Recreation

God of all goodness, as we thank you for our daily work, we thank you also for our opportunities of recreation:

for physical exercise and games,

for the companionship of books,

for the enjoyment of music and drama,

for the refreshment we find in the world of nature,

for our hobbies and holidays and rest days.

Father, may all recreation bring renewal and refreshment to our lives, so that we may be better fitted to serve you in body, mind and spirit; for Jesus Christ's sake.

Our hobbies

Father, we are grateful for our hobbies and for the interest and recreation they provide for our leisure hours.

Teach us how to use them rightly. Save us from pursuing them selfishly or allowing them to absorb too much of our time.

May they be our servants, never our masters; and may they bring pleasure and enrichment to the lives of others. In Christ's name we ask it.

129

Thank you, Lord, for hobbies which give us a chance to rest and relax, and also to develop the skills you have given us.

Help us to make the best use of our hobbies, so that they may benefit others as well as ourselves and serve your glory; for Jesus' sake.

Games

130

Lord, our games mean much to us and we thank you for them.

Help us to remember that enjoyment of the game is more important than the result, and that the game of life is more important still.

Above all, help us to remember the teaching of scripture that while bodily fitness is of certain value, spiritual fitness is of value both for the present life and the life to come.

Sportsmanship

131

Thank you, Lord God, for our games and sports and for the lessons they teach us about so many things:

> the discipline of training,
> the need of bodily fitness,

the challenge of competition,
the enjoyment of comradeship,
the importance of team spirit.
Help us, Lord, to learn these lessons and apply them to our lives; and especially teach us to show generosity in winning and good grace in losing, as befits those who honour the name of Jesus our Lord.

Holidays

132

Lord, we thank you for the rhythms of life; for day and night, for waking hours and sleep, for work and relaxation.

We thank you especially for holidays; and we pray that in this period of rest and change we may be renewed in health, refreshed in mind, and strengthened in spirit for our daily work; through Jesus Christ our Lord.

133

O God, whose will it is that all should enjoy the good things of your creation:
grant rest and renewal to those who are on holiday;
protect those who journey by land, by sea, or in the air;
and give to those who use the roads grace to exercise all care and courtesy.
We ask in the name of him who taught us to love one another, our Saviour Jesus Christ.

134

Praise God for family holidays and all the fun and excitement they provide:
the planning and preparation,
the interest and novelty of travel,
the opportunity of seeing new places, making new friends and sharing new experiences.
Lord, thank you for these things; and as on holiday we glimpse something more of your world, deepen our awareness of your vast wisdom, power, and love; for Jesus Christ's sake.

Holidays abroad

Father of all, we give you thanks for the opportunity of travelling abroad and seeing the variety of your creation.

Give us open eyes and understanding minds to delight in the fresh discoveries of each day; and in our travels may we discern those patterns of experience which show how unsparingly you give yourself to your world; through Jesus Christ our Lord.

Users of the road

136

Help me, O God, as I drive
    to love my neighbour as myself,
that I may do nothing to hurt or endanger
    any of your children.
Give to my eyes clear vision,
    and skill to my hands and feet.
Make me tranquil in mind
    and relaxed in body.
Deliver me from the spirit of rivalry,
    and from resentment at the actions of others;
and bring me safe to my journey's end,
    for Jesus Christ's sake.

137

Almighty God, our keeper and protector, grant to all who drive on the roads consideration for others.

Help them to resist the temptations of thoughtless speed and selfish law-breaking.

Give also to those who walk or cycle along the roads, or play beside them, sensible caution and care; that so, without fear or anger or disaster, we may all by your mercy come safely to our journey's end; through Jesus Christ our Lord.

The arts

138

Father, we are grateful for all the pleasure and inspiration we receive from the work of craftsmen and artists, writers and musicians, actors and singers.

As by their varied gifts they enrich our lives, so may our lives in turn give you the greater glory; through Christ our Lord.

Music makers

139

God of creation, you have made all things well and given us much to enjoy: we thank you for the gift of music, through which, far beyond words, we can feel our way towards the greater mysteries.

We thank you for the skill and sensitivity of those who by making music can give such great pleasure; and we pray that each of us may be helped to develop those talents which can be used to benefit others; through Jesus Christ our Lord.

Books

140

We are thankful, our Father, that we live in a country where books are plentifully available for enjoyment and instruction.

Help us in the choice of the books we read, that by them our minds may be expanded, our store of knowledge increased, and our lives be fashioned more closely to the pattern of truth and goodness shown us in your Son, our Saviour Jesus Christ.

A gardener's prayer

Lord, when you made Adam you gave him a garden to dig and cultivate and care for.

That is my job now in the garden you have given me.

But I don't do it alone, Lord: you and I are partners in this task.

And as I do my bit, I know that you will do yours, so that together we may make the garden a thing of beauty, a place of flowers and fruits for our enjoyment.

Thank you, Lord, for the privilege of being a worker together with you.

A time to laugh

Give us a sense of humour, Lord,
    and also things to laugh about.
Give us the grace to take a joke against ourselves
    and to see the funny side of life.
Save us from annoyance, bad temper,
    or resentfulness against our friends.
Help us to laugh even in the face of trouble;
    and fill our minds with the love of Jesus,
for his name's sake.

8   Times and Seasons

In the morning

143

For morning light and the gift of a new day,
    we praise you, our heavenly Father;
and with thankful hearts we now entrust ourselves
    and those we love into your hands;
praying that you will guard us and help us,
    guide us and strengthen us
in all that lies before us this day;
    in the name of Jesus Christ our Lord.

144

God and Father of us all, from whom alone we have the
desire and the power to live aright: grant that the clean page
of this new day may remain unspotted to the end; and that
whatever is recorded upon it by our lives may prove worthy
to be treasured in our memories; so that at the day's closing
we may present it unashamed to you; through Jesus Christ
our Lord.

145

God our Father, in your mercy
    a new day lies before us,
with its new tasks, new duties,
    and new opportunities.
Help us to face it with new faith,
    new hope and new courage;
that at its ending we may offer you
    new praise and thanksgiving,
in the name of Christ our Lord.

Almighty God, creator of the world,
when I wake up in the morning and look in the mirror
I am reminded that you made man in your own image.
Help me each day to reflect your glory
and to be part of your recreating purpose,
by the power of your Holy Spirit
and in the name of Jesus my Lord.

At evening

147

Lord, in your goodness and mercy we come to the end of another day.

Thank you for your presence with us all the day long.

Forgive us for what has been amiss: for wrongs we have done and for good things left undone.

Grant your blessing upon us as we sleep, that we may be refreshed for your service tomorrow; for Jesus' sake.

148

We thank you, our Father,
that as the day is yours, so also is the night.
And we pray that as you have cared for us
through the day that is past,
so you will have us and ours
in your safe keeping this night;
that we may find rest and refreshment,
and rise to praise and serve you
through another day; for Jesus' sake.

149

Father, we thank you for the gift of sleep.

Grant us that gift tonight and every night.

As we settle down to rest, help us to leave the cares and business of the day in your hands, to relax our minds and bodies, and to gain refreshment of spirit and renewal of strength for the work of another day; through Jesus Christ our Lord.

Jesus, my love,
must today come to an end?
Oh what joys we have shared,
just being together in silence.
My spirit is refreshed,
my strength renewed,
the peace of my soul is restored.
Jesus, my beloved, I thank you.

Bring us, O Lord, through the hours of darkness to the light
of another day; and in your great mercy guard us from every
danger of body and soul this night; for the sake of your Son
our Saviour Jesus Christ.

(A modern version of the ancient Vespers collect.)

Sunday

Almighty God, let all the voices of earth
join the voices of heaven this day
in songs of praise and thanksgiving.
For this is the day you have made.
This is the day of resurrection.
May it be for us a day of rejoicing
as we lift up our hearts and voices
with your whole Church in every place
and give honour and glory to your great name;
through Jesus Christ our Lord.

A birthday

Loving Father, we remember today — as *he* begins another
year of *his* life.

Grant that *he* may grow in wisdom and grace; and strengthen *his* trust in your goodness all *his* days; for your tender mercies' sake.

154

Heavenly Father, giver of all good things, we ask your blessing on — on this *his* birthday.

May *he* rejoice and give thanks for all your love and goodness; and through every year of *his* life may he be kept by your power and guided by your wisdom; for Jesus Christ's sake.

Wedding anniversary

155

O God our Father, we thank you today for the many blessings you have given us through our marriage;

for the love and happiness that have been ours;

for the growth you have made possible in each of us as people;

for the new dimensions you bring to our love through joys and sorrows shared.

We pray that we may never take one another for granted but may continually be renewed by your grace; and we offer the future for you to bless still more; through Jesus Christ our Lord.

156

Heavenly Father, we pray for — and — as they celebrate their wedding anniversary, that they may give thanks to you for all your goodness to them and for the love which binds them together as husband and wife.

May they remember with grateful hearts your gifts of home, family, and friends.

Help them to rejoice in their shared memories of joy and laughter, sadness and disappointment; and as they praise you for the past, may they trust you for all the days to come; in the name of Jesus our Lord.

New year

Grant, O Lord, that as the years change,
we may find rest in your unchangeableness.
May we meet this new year bravely,
sure in the faith that while men come and go,
and life changes around us,
you are ever the same,
guiding us with your wisdom
and protecting us with your love;
through Jesus Christ our Lord.

Mothering Sunday

Lord Jesus Christ, who came to share our life here on earth
and lived with your mother in the home at Nazareth: we
thank you for our homes and families, and especially today
for our mothers and all they do for us.

Bless them and keep them, O Lord; and help us all in our
family life to find our true happiness in loving and serving
one another for your sake, our Master and our Friend.

Passiontide

Father of all mankind, who in your great love
gave your only Son for the world's salvation:
give us such a vision of the cross of Jesus
and of all that he has done for us
that we may turn to you with true repentance,
acknowledging our unworthiness,
pouring contempt on all our pride,
and offering our lives back to you;
so that henceforth we may serve you
in the power and joy of his resurrection,
for the glory of your name.

Easter

We praise you, O God, for this joyful Eastertide,
as we celebrate again the great redemption
won for us by our Lord Jesus Christ
and his victory over death.
Grant us grace to enter into his triumph,
to share his risen life,
and at last to partake of his endless joy,
to the glory of his holy name.

Lord of creation and God of grace, we thank you for the yearly miracle of the spring, as the earth awakes from its winter sleep and is arrayed again in the glory of resurrection life.

May a similar miracle of grace take place in our lives this Easter. Send into our hearts the Spirit of the living Christ, to raise us to newness of life and to clothe us with the beauty of his holiness, for your honour and glory.

Pentecost

Holy Spirit of God,
great gift of our exalted Lord,
on the day of Pentecost you came to the Church
as he promised, to abide with us for ever.
Come to us in your grace and power today,
to make Jesus real to us,
to teach us more about him,
and to deepen our trust in him;
that we may be changed into his likeness
and be his witnesses in the world,
to the glory of God the Father.

Harvest

163

O God, our heavenly Father,
  we praise you for the fruits of the earth
and acknowledge that all good gifts around us
  are sent from heaven above.
Help us to receive them gratefully,
  to use them wisely,
  and to share them unselfishly,
that others may rejoice in your bounty;
  for the sake of Jesus Christ our Lord.

Christmas

164

Heavenly Father, as we prepare for Christmas,
help us, in all the busyness of these days,
to find time to think of what Christmas really means:
  of your love for the world,
  of the coming of the promised Redeemer,
  of the wonder of the Word made flesh.
May we, like Mary, treasure these things
  and ponder them in our hearts;
so that on Christmas Day we may be ready
to join in the joyful worship of the Church
  and give glory to your name.

165

Thank you, our Father, for Bethlehem and for its message
of Love incarnate, Love divine.

Shed that love abroad in our hearts and homes this
Christmas time, and help us to reflect it in our worship, in
our family life, and in all that we try to do to help those in
need.

We ask it in our Saviour's name.

Give us, our Father, this Christmas time,
   peace in our hearts,
that we may create peace in our homes
   and help to spread peace in the world,
for our Lord Jesus Christ's sake.

9 Devotional Prayers

FAMOUS PRAYERS

St Augustine of Hippo

167

O thou, from whom to be turned is to fall,
to whom to be turned is to rise,
and in whom to stand is to abide for ever;
grant us, in all our duties, thy help,
in all our perplexities, thy guidance,
in all our dangers, thy protection,
and in all our sorrows, thy peace;
through Jesus Christ our Lord.

St Benedict

168

O gracious and holy Father,
give us wisdom to perceive thee,
diligence to seek thee,
patience to wait for thee,
eyes to behold thee,
a heart to meditate upon thee,
and a life to proclaim thee;
through the power of the Spirit of Jesus Christ our Lord.

Leonine Sacramentary

169

Remember, O Lord, what thou hast wrought in us, and not
what we deserve; and, as thou hast called us to thy service,
make us worthy of our calling; through Jesus Christ our
Lord.

St Thomas Aquinas

Give us, O Lord, a steadfast heart, which no unworthy thought can drag downwards; an unconquered heart, which no tribulation can wear out; an upright heart, which no unworthy purpose may tempt aside.

Bestow upon us also, O Lord our God, understanding to know thee, diligence to seek thee, wisdom to find thee, and a faithfulness that may finally embrace thee; through Jesus Christ our Lord.

St Francis of Assisi

Lord, make us instruments of thy peace.
Where there is hatred, let us sow love;
where there is injury, pardon;
where there is doubt, faith;
where there is despair, hope;
where there is darkness, light;
where there is sadness, joy;
for thy mercy and for thy truth's sake.

St Richard of Chichester

Thanks be to thee, our Lord Jesus Christ,
for all the benefits which thou hast given us,
for all the pains and insults which thou hast borne for us.
O most merciful Redeemer, Friend, and Brother,
may we know thee more clearly,
love thee more dearly,
and follow thee more nearly,
now and for ever.

Erasmus

173

O Lord Jesus Christ, who art the way, the truth, and the life; suffer us not at any time to stray from thee, who art the way; nor to distrust thy promises, who art the truth; nor to rest in any other thing than thee, who art the life; for thou hast taught us what to believe, what to do, and wherein to take our rest.

Archbishop Cranmer

174

O Lord, who hast taught us that all our doings without charity are nothing worth: send thy Holy Ghost and pour into our hearts that most excellent gift of charity, the very bond of peace and of all virtues, without which whosoever liveth is counted dead before thee. Grant this for thine only Son Jesus Christ's sake.

St Ignatius Loyola

175

Teach us, good Lord, to serve thee as thou deservest:
to give and not to count the cost;
to fight and not to heed the wounds;
to toil and not to seek for rest;
to labour and not to ask for any reward
save that of knowing that we do thy will;
through Jesus Christ our Lord.

Sir Francis Drake

176

O Lord God, when thou givest to thy servants to endeavour any great matter, grant us also to know that it is not the beginning, but the continuing of the same unto the end,

63

until it be thoroughly finished, which yieldeth the true glory; through him who for the finishing of thy work laid down his life, our Redeemer Jesus Christ.

Cardinal Newman

177

O Lord, support us all the day long of this troublous life, until the shades lengthen, and the evening comes, and the busy world is hushed, the fever of life is over, and our work is done. Then, Lord, in thy mercy, grant us safe lodging, a holy rest, and peace at the last; through Jesus Christ our Lord.

PRAYERS OLD AND NEW

The holiness of God

178

O God, our Judge and Saviour, set before us the vision of thy purity, and let us see our sins in the light of thy holiness. Pierce our self-contentment with the shafts of thy burning love, and let that love consume in us all that hinders us from perfect service of thy cause; for as thy holiness is our judgement, so are thy wounds our salvation.

Penitence

179

If my soul has turned perversely to the dark;
if I have left some brother wounded by the way;
if I have preferred my aims to thine;
if I have been impatient and would not wait;

if I have marred the pattern drawn out for my life;
if I have cost tears to those I love;
if my heart has murmured against thy will:
    O Lord, in thy mercy forgive.

Grace

180

O God our Father, let us find grace in thy sight so as to have grace to serve thee acceptably with reverence and godly fear; and further grace not to receive thy grace in vain, nor to neglect it and fall from it, but to stir it up and grow in it, and to persevere in it unto the end of our lives; through Jesus Christ our Lord.

Faith

181

O Lord, strengthen the faith of us who believe, and sow the seed of faith in the hearts of those who lack it.

    Give us grace to show our faith by our works; teach us to walk by faith, in reliance on thy promises; and enable us to fight the good fight of faith, that by faith we may overcome the world; through our Lord and Saviour Jesus Christ.

Renewal

182

    Almighty God, who in Christ makest all things new:
    transform the poverty of our nature
    into the riches of thy grace;
    that by the renewal of our lives
    thy glory may be revealed;
    through Jesus Christ our Lord.

Inward peace

183

Most loving Father, who willest us to give thanks for all things, to dread nothing but the loss of thee, and to cast all our care on thee who carest for us: preserve us from faithless fears and worldly anxieties, and grant that no clouds of this mortal life may hide us from the light of thy love which is immortal, and which thou hast manifested to us in thy Son, Jesus Christ our Lord.

Guidance

184

O God, by whom the meek are guided in judgement, and light riseth up in darkness for the godly: grant us, in all our doubts and uncertainties, the grace to ask what thou wouldest have us to do; that the Spirit of wisdom may save us from all false choices, and that in thy light we may see light and may not stumble; through Jesus Christ our Lord.

Sympathy

185

Grant us grace, our Father, not to pass by suffering or joy without eyes to see them.

Give us understanding and sympathy, and guard us from selfishness.

Help us to enter into the joys and sorrows of others; and use us to gladden and strengthen those who are weak and suffering; for the sake of Christ our Lord.

Thankfulness

186

Forgive me, Lord, for a mind
that turns so readily to weigh my troubles,
 so seldom to count my blessings.

Teach me the practice of recollection,
   the habit of thankfulness,
   the art of praise.
And may I deal as generously with others
   as you deal with me;
for Jesus Christ's sake.

Love for God

187

O God, we love you
   because you first loved us.
Yet our love for you is so weak
   while your love for us is so strong.
Teach us more of your love,
   that we may love you better;
and help us to show our love for you
   by our love for others,
even as you love both them and us,
   in Jesus Christ our Lord.

Faith for all times

188

We thank you, our Father, that our times are in your hand:
   our times of adversity as well as of prosperity;
   our times of sorrow as well as of joy;
   our times of sickness as well as of health.
Help us to trust you at all times,
knowing that amid life's changing scenes
your love for us is unchanging
and will never let us go.
We ask it in the name of Jesus Christ our Lord.

Only one

Lord, I am only one,
    but I *am* one.
I cannot do everything,
    but I *can* do something.
What I can do,
    I *ought* to do;
and what I ought to do
    I *will* do,
in the strength of Christ my Lord.

Looking at life

Heavenly Father, in our journey through life
teach us to look back with gratitude
    and count our blessings;
to look around with compassion
    and serve those in need;
to look forward with confidence
    and trust you for all that's to come;
in the faith of Jesus Christ our Lord.

The pattern of life

Jesus, alone on the mountain,
deep in solitude and prayer:
    teach me the same.
Jesus, busy in the market place,
close to the people you love:
    teach me the same.
Jesus, you know the need
for both solitude and work:
    teach me the same,
so that I may grow to be more like you
in love and prayer.

Jesus my friend

Jesus, my friend, you are always there,
   even when things go wrong.
You are not a friend who is around
   only on good days;
you are very close on the bad ones too,
   and I thank you for that.
I have much that needs forgiving,
   and you have forgiven me.
So once again I am free,
   no longer a slave to myself
   but a willing servant to you.
Thank you, thank you, so much.

Poverty

O holy poverty, friend of our Lord,
   dwell within my heart, I pray.
Let it be not only the outward
   but more so the inward,
   that of the spirit, pure and divine.
O holy poverty,
   teach me to be Christlike,
   an imitation of him whom I love.

Lord, have mercy

Lord, have mercy on me, a miserable sinner,
full of selfishness and pride.
Stretch forth your hand, O Lord,
and rid me of this cancerous growth.

Lord, have mercy, Lord, have mercy,
a hateful person that I am.

Say the word only, and I shall be healed;
rid me of this hate that is within me.

Lord, have mercy, cast out this demon,
cast it into the depth of the sea,
rid me of it now and for ever:
only you can save me.

Dedication

195

Jesus, you have died for me,
    so let me live for you.
And as you still live, O Lord,
    may I die to self,
so that I may serve you
    wholeheartedly.

10 Arrow prayers

Lord Jesus Christ, Son of God,
be merciful to me, a sinner.

  (The Jesus Prayer)

Dear God, be good to me:
the sea is so wide and my boat is so small.

  (Prayer of Breton fishermen)

Lord, you have given so much to me: give me one thing
more, a grateful heart.

  (After George Herbert)

Let my chief end, O God, be to glorify you, and to enjoy you
for ever.

  (From the Shorter Catechism)

Lord, you have so much time for me:
let me have more time for you.

Lord, make me what you want me to be,
that I may accomplish what you want me to do.

Lord, what we know not, teach us;
what we have not, give us;
what we are not, make us.

Lord, grant that we who most frequently speak your name,
may also be those who most readily obey your will.

So keep us in your fear, O Lord, that we may be free from
every other fear.

Lord, give us work till our life shall end,
and give us life till our work is done.

O Lord of the Church,
make us the Church of the Lord.

(George Appleton)

Lord, renew our spirits, that our work may not be to us a burden but a delight.

(Benjamin Jenks)

Help us, O God, to be masters of ourselves,
that we may become the servants of others.

O God, from whom we come and to whom we shall return:
be with us now and at the hour of our death.

Index of Sources

61	Andrew Warner	96	Richard Harries
62	Editor	97	Richard Harries
63	ECUSA*	98	Sister Phyllis, CSF
64	Helen Lee	99	Editor
65	Adapted from William Barclay	100	Editor
66	Mothers' Union	101	Editor
67	Editor	102	Richard Bewes
68	Editor	103	Editor
69	Editor (adapted)	104	Andrew Warner
70	Andrew Warner	105	Editor
71	Richard Bewes	106	Editor
72	Llewellyn Cumings	107	ECUSA*
73	Mothers' Union	108	Editor
74	Patricia Mitchell	109	F. W. Street*
75	Llewellyn Cumings	110	Llewellyn Cumings
76	Susan Williams	111	Editor
77	Editor	112	ECUSA
78	Editor (adapted)	113	Editor
79	Editor	114	Church Missionary Society
80	Editor	115	Church Missionary Society
81	Richard Bewes	116	Church Missionary Society
82	Helen Lee	117	Helen Lee
83	Editor (adapted)	118	Editor
84	D. W. Grundy	119	Editor
85	Editor	120	Editor
86	Adapted from William Barclay	121	Editor
87	Joy Whyte*	122	ECUSA
88	Richard Harries	123	Timothy Dudley-Smith
89	Richard Bewes	124	Timothy Dudley-Smith
90	Editor	125	Editor
91	Llewellyn Cumings	126	Llewellyn Cumings
92	Sister Phyllis, CSF	127	Editor
93	Richard Harries	128	Editor
94	Editor	129	Llewellyn Cumings
95	Richard Harries		

Index of Subjects

The numbers are those prefixed to the prayers.

Also by
FRANK COLQUHOUN in

Tri∧ngle

Prayers that Live

Canon Colquhoun has selected for devotional
commentary thirty familiar and well-loved prayers.
Varying considerably in their origin, date, style and
themes, they all have in common the power to touch
our lives at a deep level, and.to echo the needs and
longings of men and women everywhere, and at all
times.

'What Frank Colquhoun's *Hymns that Live* can do for
our singing, this book can do for our praying. It is
designed to help ordinary Christians to appreciate what
they may hear in church, and to make these prayers
their own.'
C of E Newspaper

'Another seam of gold in the mine of Christian
devotion.'
Baptist Times

More Christian paperbacks from

TRIANGLE

Shelagh Brown (ed.)

MARRIED TO THE CHURCH?
Ten clergy wives write frankly about themselves and
their marriages.
'A very human story. It brings a new understanding
and greater respect for clergy wives.' *Church News*

Amy Carmichael

CANDLES IN THE DARK
The author shares the riches of her spiritual
experience in letters of counsel and encouragement.
'Gems of love and trust.' *Church Times*

WHISPERS OF HIS POWER
Daily devotional readings.
'The value of these letters lies in the deep spirituality
and compassion which shine out of them.' *Christian
Herald*

Brenda Courtie

NOT QUITE HEAVEN
A heart-warming account by a Liverpool housewife of
deepening Christian experience through everyday life.

Margaret Cundiff

'Margaret Cundiff is communicating God's love and joyousness all the time.' *C of E Newspaper*

CALLED TO BE ME
Lively reminiscences of a deaconess in a Yorkshire parish.
'Realistic and hilarious' *Christian Bookseller*
With line illustrations

FOLLOWING ON
Another enjoyable invitation to meet the people who share in the life of this busy woman minister.
With line illustrations

Richard Foster

FREEDOM OF SIMPLICITY
A joyous call to a neglected discipline.
'Outstanding quality' *Baptist Times*

Joyce Landorf

IRREGULAR PEOPLE
How to cope with someone close who constantly upsets you. Written by one of America's leading Christian counsellors.

Morris Maddocks

THE CHRISTIAN ADVENTURE
Bible studies on God's call to commitment, prayer, loving and witness.
'A timely, pastoral and spiritually affecting book'
Church Times

Linette Martin

PRACTICAL PRAYING
Guidance for those who find praying difficult.

Charles Ohlrich

THE SUFFERING GOD
Foreword by Sir Norman Anderson
A small gem of a book about pain and a loving God.

Juan Carlos Ortiz

LIVING WITH JESUS TODAY
Jesus is not to be kept in a separate compartment but
lives in every moment of our lives.
'This book comes as light at the end of the tunnel'
Today

John Polkinghorne

THE WAY THE WORLD IS
The Christian perspective of a scientist.
'Every minister should read it. And it is just the thing
to give to sixth formers.' *Expository Times*

Eugenia Price

THE BURDEN IS LIGHT
This best-selling author tells how she came to know
Christ.

GETTING THROUGH THE NIGHT
Comfort and help for those who mourn.

J. Oswald Sanders

THE INCOMPARABLE CHRIST
A classic devotional study of Christ's life and work.

Keith Sutton

THE PEOPLE OF GOD
A look at the practical and spiritual implications of
being God's people in the world today.

John Woolmer

GROWING UP TO SALVATION
An exploration of the many ways by which the believer
may mature into an effective disciple.
'A thoroughly practical starter on Christian living.'
Church Times